LEARNING ABOUT THE
WESTWARD EXPANSION
WITH ARTS & CRAFTS

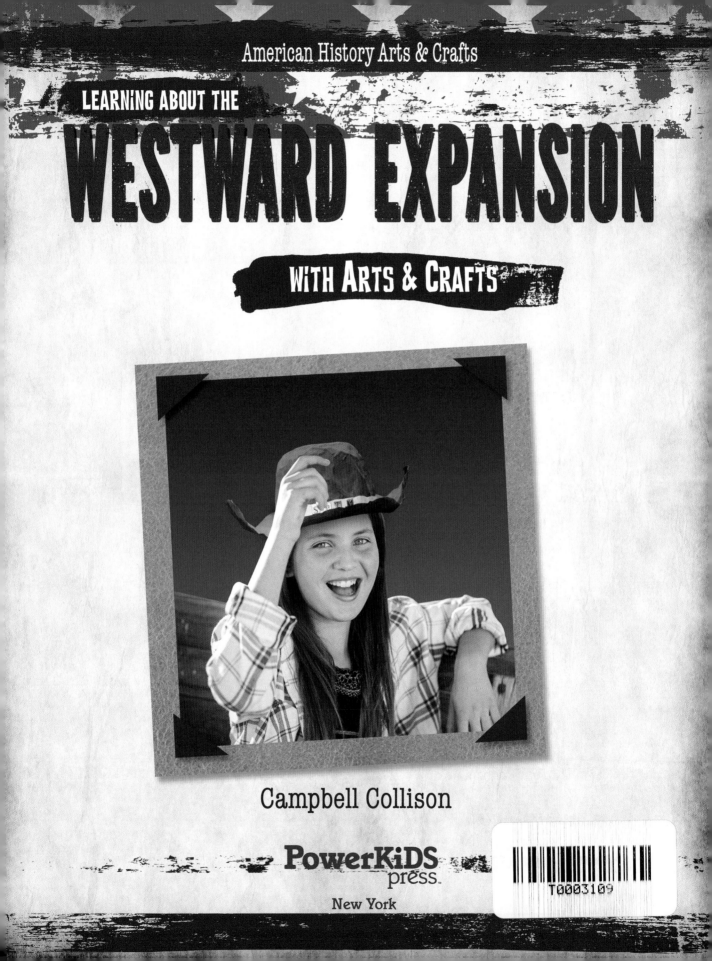

Campbell Collison

PowerKiDS press

New York

T0003109

Published in 2015 by **The Rosen Publishing Group, Inc.**
29 East 21st Street, New York, NY 10010

Library of Congress Cataloging-in-Publication-Data

Collison, Campbell.
 Learning about the westward expansion with arts & crafts / Campbell Collison.
    pages cm. — (American history arts & crafts)
 Includes index.
ISBN 978-1-4777-5884-7 (pbk.)
ISBN 978-1-4777-5885-4 (6 pack)
ISBN 978-1-4777-5882-3 (library binding)
1. Frontier and pioneer life—West (U.S.)—Study and teaching—Activity programs—Juvenile literature.
2. United States—Territorial expansion—Study and teaching—Activity programs—Juvenile literature.
3. West (U.S.)—History—Study and teaching—Activity programs—Juvenile literature. I. Title. II. Title:
Learning about the westward expansion with arts and crafts.
E179.5.C56 2015
978'.02—dc23

2014033932

Copyright © 2015 by The Rosen Publishing Group, Inc.

Developed and produced for Rosen by BlueAppleWorks Inc.
Art Director: T. J. Choleva
Managing Editor for BlueAppleWorks: Melissa McClellan
Photo Research: Jane Reid
Editor: Joanne Randolph
Craft Consultant: Jerrie McClellan

Acknowledgments:
The authors thank: Charles Sable, Curator of Decorative Arts at The Henry Ford, Dearborn, MI; Audrey Sterk, Audrey Sterk Design, Nantucket, MA; Matthew Range, Marketing Director, Hatco Inc., Garland, TX; Carlyn Hammons, Historian for Federal Programs, Texas Historical Commission, Austin, TX; Laura Poresky, Period Clothing Supervisor, Living History Farms, Urbandale, IA; Pamela Eddy, Park Ranger and Historical Interpreter, Cumberland Gap National Park; Carol Borneman, Park Ranger, Cumberland Gap National Park; Mark Engler, Park Ranger, Homestead National Monument of America, Beatrice, NE; Blake Bell, Historian, Homestead National Monument of America; Jeremy Johnston, Curator of the Buffalo Bill Museum and Western American History, Buffalo Bill Center of the West, Cody, WY; Ed Allen, Historian, Marshall Gold Discovery State Park, Coloma, CA; Todd Thibodeau, Planning and Grants Manager, Wyoming State Parks, Historic Sites & Trails. We also wish to thank these institutions: The Buffalo Bill Center of the West, Cody, WY; The Cherokee Heritage Center, Park Hill, OK; the Texas Historical Commission, Austin, TX; the Library of Congress and National Archives, Washington, D.C.Editor's Note: Campbell Collison is a pseudonym for Janis Campbell and Cathy Collison. The two have been writing for young readers for more than 20 years. They compiled the editorial content to accompany the arts and crafts created by the Blue Apple Works editorial team.

Photo & Illustration Credits:
Cover T. J. Choleva (Bambi L. Dingman/Dreamstime, justasc/Shutterstock); cover side images top to bottom (janr34/Shutterstock, Tmcnem/Dreamstime, Olivier Le Queinec/Dreamstime); title page Andy Dean Photography/Shutterstock; sidebars Dariusz Pawlowski/Shutterstock; map p. 4 T. J. Choleva; p. 4 bottom Emanuel Leutze/Public Domain; p. 5 AKaiser/Shutterstock; p.6–7 bottom Stratosphere/Creative Commons; p. 6 top William Tylee Ranney/Public Domain; p. 7, 10, 12 left, 23, 26 left, 27 right Charles Marion Russell/Public Domain; p. 7 right Chester Harding/Public Domain; p. 8 left © Maglara/Dreamstime; p. 8–9, 16–17, 20–21, 24–25 Austen Photography; p. 10 top Thure de Thulstrup/Public Domain; p. 11 Edgar Samuel Paxson/Public Domain; p. 12 top United States Department of Agriculture/Public Domain; p. 13 left Carl Nebel/Public Domain; p.13 right Kushal Bose/Shutterstock; p. 14, 15 left, 15 right Alfred Jacob Miller/Public Domain; p. 14 top William Tylee Ranney/Public Domain; p. 18 top G.F. Nesbitt & Co/Public Domain; p. 18–19 bottom, 19, right, 20 left Library of Congress/Public Domain; p. 22 left Charles J. Belden/Public Domain; p. 22 top, 29 Public Domain; p. 24 left Arthur Rothstein/Library of Congress/Public Domain; p.26–27 bottom Jason Patrick Ross/Shutterstock; p. 27 left Sergei Bachlakov/Shutterstock; p. 28 Thomas Hill/Public Domain; p. 29 T. J. Choleva (D. F. Barry/Public Domain)

Manufactured in the United States of America
CPSIA Compliance Information: Batch #CW15PK For Further Information contact: Rosen Publishing, New York, New York at 1-800-237-9932

Table of Contents

A Nation on the Move   4

Into the Wilderness   6

Craft to Make: Spatter Painting   8

The Louisiana Purchase   10

Texas Tale   12

The Oregon Trail   14

Craft to Make: Cowboy Hat   16

Gold Rush!   18

Craft to Make: Gold Nugget Pouch   20

Tough First Years   22

Craft to Make: Woven Basket   24

Removed by Force   26

Settled Land   28

Glossary   30

For More Information   31

Index   32

A Nation on the Move

Thirteen colonies once defined the America that was known to the citizens who had settled and built their farms, businesses, and towns east of the Appalachian Mountains. Few knew about the rest of the lands west, where native nations were thriving. In fact, Great Britain ruled in the Proclamation of 1763 that no one was allowed to **claim** – or even cross – that mountain border, and the land immediately west belonged to the Native Americans. After the Revolutionary War, the stage was set for western expansion in a series of land purchases that pushed out the borders of those former colonies in every direction. The first borders claimed were west to the Mississippi River, north to the Canadian border, and south to Florida.

This map shows when different land areas were claimed after the Revolutionary War.

1818
1846
1803
1848
1803
1783
1783
1776
1853
1845
1819

Original States – 1776

Old Northwest – 1783

Old Southwest – 1783

Louisiana Purchase – 1803

Red River Basin – 1818

Spanish Florida – 1819

Texas Annexation – 1845

Oregon Country – 1846

Mexican Cession – 1848

Gadsden Purchase – 1853

Major Changes

Many new laws were passed and treaties signed by the United States government, leading to the formation of the United States as we know it today. Read about the key events below.

UNITED STATES EXPANSION — KEY EVENTS — THE DAILY NEWSPAPER

TERRITORY TIME

In 1785, Congress passed the **Ordinance** of 1785. It allowed for the sale of land in what had been regions claimed by the Native American nations. Settlers bought land in what was then called the Northwest **Territory**, which is now part of the Midwest and Great Lakes regions.

WAR WITH MEXICO

The U.S.-Mexican War from 1846-1848 shaped the borders of the southwest U.S., with Mexico losing vast territory and the United States expanding its land holdings to present-day Texas west to California.

THE LOUISIANA PURCHASE

In 1803, the United States bought a huge parcel of land from France, a vast land buy that stretched north to Canada, west to present-day Montana and down to the Gulf of Mexico.

NORTHERN BORDER TREATIES

The **Treaty** of 1818 with the United Kingdom of Great Britain created what we now know as the northern border in parts of the U.S. with Canada. In 1846, that boundary became more complete with the Oregon Treaty, with the British getting Vancouver Island and the U.S. getting lands south of the 49th parallel.

TRANSCONTINENTAL TREATY

With the Adams-Onis Treaty of 1819, Spain gave up Florida and all of its land in the Pacific Northwest.

GADSEN PURCHASE

For $10 million, James Gadsen, a railroad contractor, bought a piece of land from Mexico for President Franklin Pierce, which added areas of what is now Arizona and New Mexico.

SPECIAL ISSUE

FRONTIER FACT

The United States population grew from about 5.3 million in 1800 to 9.6 million by 1820.

WAR WITH MEXICO

1846-1848

James Gadsen

Into the Wilderness

Rules of the British Proclamation of 1763 could not be enforced as on occasions individual settlers pushed west anyway.

A leader in forging west, and creating a new path to open up new lands, was Daniel Boone. As early as 1767, the legendary explorer had already discovered the Cumberland Gap in the Appalachian Mountains, which led from North Carolina into what is now Kentucky.

Daniel Boone first reached Kentucky in the fall of 1767 while on a long hunting trip.

In 1775 Boone and a company of about 30 men carved out a wide trail from a narrow path which became known as the Wilderness Road. Boone and his men crossed into Kentucky where they founded the village of Boonesborough, one of the first American **settlements** west of the Appalachians.

By 1810, the Wilderness Road, cut for travel by Boone and his men, was traveled by 300,000 **pioneers**.

The Cumberland Gap in the Appalachian Mountains is now part of the Cumberland Gap National Historical Park.

Up to the Northwest, Down to the Southeast

Other parts of the United States were also due for expansion. When the Treaty of Paris ended the American Revolution in 1783, it added land that is now the Great Lakes region to United States territory. Settlers began to push into the area by the Ohio River.

Meanwhile, the southeastern parts of the United States also drew settlers in greater numbers. By 1821, the United States acquired Florida as well as Alabama and Mississippi. The attractive climate and conditions for farming drew many people to settle in the region.

Daniel Boone had many talents. He also owned a tavern and was a blacksmith.

Settlers often traveled to new territories in groups for protection.

Craft to Make:

Spatter Painting

Early settlers did not have many resources at first, but tried to make their homes and furniture look pretty. Spatter painting was a popular technique used to decorate floors, walls, and furniture. This decorating style was inspired by spatterware ceramics from England, which was popular and accessible to all.

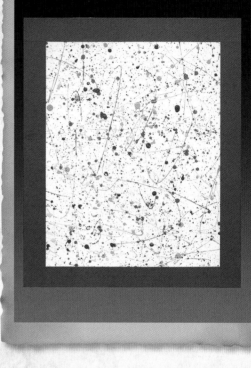

Spatter pottery was produced by English potters during the 1800s for the American market. It was the most popular of the hand-decorated wares in that period.

What You Will Need

- Heavy paper or bristol board
- Newspaper
- Acrylic paint
- Brushes, toothbrush
- Small cups
- Colored tape
- String

Step One

This craft can be messy, so it is best if you do it outside. If you have an old shirt, wear it to protect your clothes. Spread out some newspapers to work on. Put your paper on the newspaper. Prepare your paints by mixing a small amount of water with the paint in small cups. If you want a colored background, paint it first.

Step Two

Time to splatter. Dip your paintbrush into the paint, and then while holding the brush about 2 inches (5 cm) above the paper, shake, or flick, the brush. You can also tap the brush to create smaller splatters. Do this with different colors of paint. Experiment with the force of the flick and the distance you hold the brush from the paper. Try a toothbrush. Have fun!

Step Three

Leave your painting to dry. Make a nice frame for your work of art. Cut four pieces of colored tape and place along each side of the painting when it is dry. Wrap the extra behind the painting.

Tape a small piece of string on the back so that you can display your work of art.

The Louisiana Purchase

French explorers had settled a huge territory in 1682, naming it Louisiana for King Louis XIV. In the next 120 years, the land had different owners but ended up being owned by France once more. Finally, French ruler Napoleon Bonaparte decided to sell the vast land of 828,000 square miles (2,144,000 square kilometers) to the United States for $15 million. In 1803, President Thomas Jefferson agreed to the deal. Acquiring the land doubled the size of the United States and led to one of the most remarkable explorations in American history.

The ceremony at Place d'Armes in New Orleans marked the transfer of Louisiana to the United States in 1804.

The newly acquired territory was mostly untouched by white men. It was teeming with wildlife and natural resources.

Lewis and Clark

President Thomas Jefferson wanted to know about the Native American people, land, plants, animals, and climate that existed beyond the Mississippi River. He sent Meriwether Lewis and William Clark on an ambitious journey with hopes of discovering a river trade route that extended to the Pacific Ocean. President Jefferson requested that the explorers keep detailed records of their discoveries. Their expedition took nearly two and a half years and covered more than 8,000 miles (12,875 kilometres). They never found the river route, but they did reach the Pacific, mapping and establishing American presence for a legal claim to the vast land.

Sacagawea was very helpful as Lewis and Clark established trade relations with at least two dozen Native American nations during their journey.

Texas Tale

Texas is a big, bold state with an equally big, bold history. By 1821, Mexico had won its independence from Spain. Part of the new Republic of Mexico included an area called Texas, which was a rough and tumble place with

Many American settlers moved to Mexican territory to raise their herds on abundant land.

settlements spread far and wide, making it a challenge to control. To increase the population and make the region safer, Mexican officials welcomed American settlers. Settlers flocked to the territory, and soon there were thousands of Americans. In 1833, Antonio López de Santa Anna, a former military leader, became the ruler of Mexico. He introduced many new laws that the settlers did not like. American settlers rebelled, setting off the Texas Revolution. By 1844 Texas had been recognized as an American territory. The following year, in December 1845, Texas became the 28th state.

Early settlements on Mexican territory were rough and mostly lawless places.

Texas, United States

Meanwhile, tensions continued to exist between Mexico and the United States, finally spilling over into war with Mexico in 1846. The war ended in 1848, giving the United States a significant boost in land. The United States paid Mexico $15 million for the disputed land, and Mexico gave up almost half of its territory, including any claims to Texas, plus what would be California, Utah, and New Mexico, and other southwest lands. President Polk, who had been promoting **westward expansion**, ended up gaining more land for the United States than ever before.

REMEMBER THE ALAMO?

The most important battle of the Texas Revolution took place at the Alamo, a mission and fort in San Antonio. There, a group of about 200 men stood up to nearly 2,000 soldiers from the Mexican army. Against unbelievable odds, the brave fighters held the fort for 13 days before the compound was overrun. Almost all of the Texas fighters were lost in the battle. The defenders' heroic fight inspired their fellow Texans to "Remember the Alamo," when they exacted their revenge two months later. Texas soldiers pulled off a surprise attack on Mexican General Santa Anna and his men and captured the leader.

The proud Spanish heritage is evident still today in Texas. San Antonio, with its beautiful missions established by Spaniards, is one of the best known cities in the region.

The American army captured Mexico City, and the war ended in a victory for the United States.

The Oregon Trail

Even in the early 1800s, word began to spread east about the rich land in Oregon. It was originally only reached by ships coming from the Pacific Ocean. After Lewis and Clark's journey, more fur trappers headed west.

Families of settlers had high expectations of finding rich farmlands in Oregon.

An important pass, or a gap between mountains, was found through the previously impassable Rocky Mountains. By the 1830s, wagons began to follow the trail through the pass across the Rockies. A decade later, families were headed off on the trail to make homes and farm the Oregon land. In 1843, a wagon train of 800 people, more than 500 wagons, and 1,000 cattle made the journey from Independence, Missouri, where wagons were loaded. That success led to the Oregon Trail emigration.

Altogether, about 400,000 settlers and other migrants traveled the Oregon Trail in the 1800s.

On the Road

The trail was tough. In fact, men, women, and children usually walked beside the wagons, which needed to be filled with supplies, including giant barrels of water for the long trip. Oxen pulled the wagon's load, sometimes up to 2,500 pounds (1,134 kilograms), as it was too heavy for horses.

The distance covered would often just be 5 miles (8 km) a day. Sometimes 15 to 20 miles (24–32 km) could be possible, but only when weather cooperated and there were no obstacles. It was essential to cross the Rockies before snowstorms set in, as early as October.

DANGERS BEFALL PIONEERS

Crossing the Oregon Trail was a dangerous journey. Although some tales of Indian attacks scared the travellers, attacks were actually rare. In fact, Native American nations established trade along the trail. Pioneers faced far greater dangers in diseases like cholera, which was from contaminated or dirty water. Other diseases like malaria, from infected mosquito bites, and illnesses from exhaustion and even starvation took lives of settlers. River crossings were treacherous, as most pioneers did not know how to swim.

Storms in the mountains often caused delays in travel time and many other hardships.

During the first years, it took from about 160 to 170 days to complete the Oregon Trail journey.

Craft to Make:

Cowboy Hat

The pioneer's wardrobe was handmade and practical. Later as the western frontier developed, ranchers had a different look due to their jobs of riding horses and rounding up cattle. A cowboy would need chaps, the protective leatherwear worn over pants, riding boots, and of course, a cowboy hat.

Cowboys wore hats year-round for protection from the sun, rain, and snow.

What You Will Need

- Bowl that fits your head
- Newspaper, plain paper
- Tape and glue
- Scissors
- Paint and brush
- Twine or leather strip
- Decorative fasteners

Step One

Place a large piece of newspaper over an upturned bowl. Press the paper down and tape along the edge. Tear paper or newspapers into fairly large strips. Make papier-mâché paste by mixing approximately 2 parts white glue with 1 part water. Dip a piece of paper into the paste. Shake off excess paste, and lay the piece on the bowl. Smooth out the paper with your finger. Continue until you have covered the bowl. Let it dry.

Step Two

Take the hat off the bowl. Trim the paper that is extending from the tape to about one inch (2.5 cm) of the edge.

Step Three

Cut two hat brims from large pieces of paper or newspaper. Put a smaller bowl than you used earlier, and trace around the edge of the bowl. Cut this inner circle out of the paper. Clip into the circle eight times.

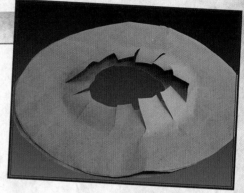

Step Four

Put one brim over the hat and slide into place. Glue the tabs into place. Turn the hat over, and line up the bottom brim with the top brim. Glue the tabs of the bottom brim inside the hat.

Step Five

Glue the two brims together using a brush to spread the glue around. Roll the edges of the hat up, and place objects to hold them in place as the hat brim is drying.

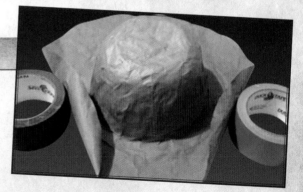

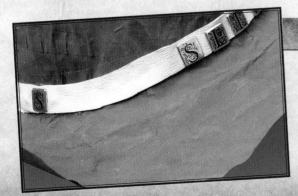

Step Six

Paint your hat and leave it to dry. Decorate with decorative fasteners. Tie a piece of thick twine or a leather strip above the brim.

Gold Rush!

What began as a simple building of a sawmill in California became a history-changing event. James W. Marshall discovered gold in 1848 on the American River in California, near the sawmill that he was building for John Sutter, who owned the property.

Like a match to a fire, the discovery lit up a mass movement that changed California and the West. Within a year, the population of white settlers in California, which was about 8,000 to 12,000 people, grew by 90,000 people.

As the boom continued, California's population grew so fast that, by 1850, it became a state. By 1854, the rush was over, and finding gold became rare. The sudden growth in population caused many more towns to be built throughout California and the few existing towns to be greatly expanded.

The California Gold Rush brought rapid growth to San Francisco. The city became the largest city on the West Coast at the time.

Shantytowns

This discovery also brought different people than the pioneers to the West, including miners, gold-panners, and anyone who thought he could make his fortune by finding the precious mineral. They believed they weren't here to stay or farm, but to get rich! They also wanted to get rich quickly if they could. Some did. At a time when factory workers in the East were earning $1 a day, the early and lucky prospectors might make $10 or even $20 a day. Others fell prey to disease, illness, and crime. Life in tent towns, or later shantytowns (a shanty being a shack), was rough and tough. The towns were mainly filled with men and filled with crime.

PANNING FOR GOLD

Panning for gold was not easy work. Prospectors had to wade into a stream with a shallow metal pan, shaped like a pie plate. They filled the pan with small gravel or sand and dipped it into the stream with a bit of a tilt, swirling the sand around slowly in a circle. Lighter sand and gravel rose up and could be sifted out. Prospectors had to sift the gravel carefully, as they did not want to lose any gold. Gold, being heavier than sand and gravel, ended up in the bottom of the pan. If they were lucky enough to find a nugget, they put it in their leather pouch.

The year 1849 was the big boom year as the word traveled east. Thousands of the gold-seekers that arrived that year were called '49ers.

Craft to Make:

Gold Nugget Pouch

You could call it the prospector's wallet. As gold seekers moved west to California to strike it rich, many began carrying their collected nuggets in a small buckskin pouch or sack, usually called a "poke" by the prospectors. The buckskin sack might also be used to carry money. Sometimes payment for goods could be made right from the pouch's nuggets or gold dust.

*Prospectors carried the gold flakes and nuggets they found on their **claims** in leather pouches.*

What You Will Need

- Piece of suede or felt
- Scissors
- Marker
- Tape
- Thick twine or strip of suede
- Small pebbles
- Acrylic gold paint
- Brush

Step One

Start with a 9-inch (23 cm) square piece of felt or suede. Cut the corners off to create a circle. Make dots on your felt, ½ inch (1 cm) from the edge, about ½ inch (1 cm) apart.

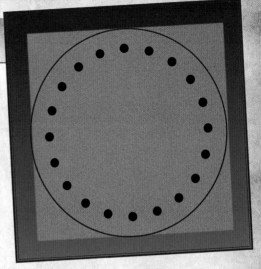

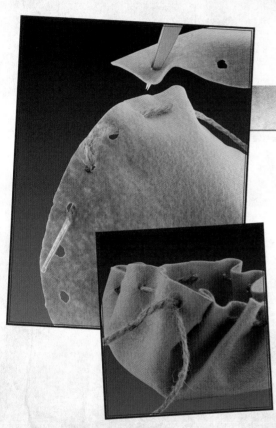

Step Two

Use your scissors to poke a hole through each dot. Cut a piece of twine 42 inches (106 cm) long. Wrap a piece of tape around the end of the twine. Thread your twine in and out through each hole leading with the taped end. When you are finished, pull each end of the twine tight to close your pouch.

Step Three

Arrange your rocks on a piece of paper. Paint them with the gold paint. Leave them to dry. When they are dry, put them in your pouch.

Tough First Years

Can you picture making a house of grass, dirt, and mud, or in other words, sod?

Early homesteaders built houses out of the sod on the treeless land of the prairies.

That was just one of the ways settlers built a home to claim and farm lands in the west. The Homestead Act of 1862, signed by President Abraham Lincoln, offered a "free chance" to men and women to establish a home (and even citizenship) by giving them 160 acres (65 ha) of free land. What was the challenge? To own and keep the land, a family had to settle there for at least five years with at least 10 acres (4 ha) of that land farmed.

That was no easy task. A huge factor in success or failure was weather. Weather could ruin a crop and so could prairie fires. Drought in the summer and freezing blizzards in the winter created unbearable conditions for some. Many returned to cities or went on to work in the growing towns in some kind of other business.

Freezing blizzards during winters caused much hardship for farmers and their livestock.

Life at a Homestead

Everyone worked at a homestead, including the children, from dawn to dusk. Plowing, planting, and harvesting crops was hard work and so were everyday chores. Chores included getting water from a creek or a well, cooking over a fire, or later a coal-burning stove, and sewing quilts and clothes by hand. Even making a fire was work. If wood or coal wasn't available, families might make hay twists — twisting hay from the **prairie** grasses together to make logs.

Early settlers occasionally clashed with the Native American nations remaining on the land, although much of the Native Americans had been pushed west and removed from the **homesteading** areas by 1862. Settlers did hunt bison, further depleting the hunting grounds of Native Americans as well.

> **DID YOU KNOW ?**
>
> Over 1.6 million people claimed 270 million acres (109 million ha) through homesteading. Of the original homesteaders, only 45 percent of those who filed claims stayed on their land for five years.

Native Americans did not welcome the many settlers. Besides taking up the land for farming, the settlers hunted bison that Plains nations depended on.

Craft to Make:

Woven Basket

Basket making is a tradition that is common to every ethnicity and cultural tradition. Not only the Native Americans had their basket-making traditions, but also the British. All of the many immigrants brought their skills and traditions of basketry, or basket making, with them wherever they settled, too. Baskets were a common and useful household item for carrying and storing goods, and were used in all ranks of society.

Settlers wove their own baskets for daily use.

What You Will Need

- Newspapers
- Glue or glue stick and masking tape
- Scissors
- Paints and brushes

Step One

Take one sheet of newspaper, and fold it over and over until you are left with a strip between 1/2 inch to 1 inch (1.3–2.5 cm) wide. Rub your hand along it to flatten it as much as you can. Use a glue stick to glue down the open edge. Repeat this until you have 12 long strips.

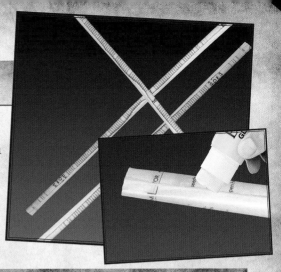

Step Two

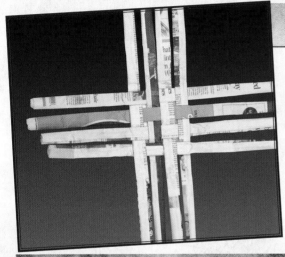

Lay out four strips vertically and four strips horizontally. Weave the strips over and under four times. You now have the bottom of the basket. Fold each strip towards the center of the basket. Tape the pieces in place.

Step Three

Take one of the remaining four strips. At the bottom, start weaving that strip in and out along the bottom. When you have gone through all the side pieces, tape it in place. Repeat for the other three pieces.

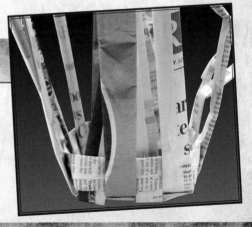

Step Four

Cut the end of each strip so that there is about 2 inches (5 cm) left above the last horizontal weave. Fold the tops of the strips into the basket, and tape them in place. For the strips that are already on the inside, fold them in and tape in place. Paint your basket inside and out.

Removed by Force

One of the most painful chapters in American history is the treatment, especially during the westward expansion years, of the Native American peoples.

As white settlers pushed west, the government pushed its policies as well. A major impact came from a landmark policy, the Indian Removal Act, in 1830. It dictated that a majority of the tribes, especially those in the South, be removed and sent west of the Mississippi River.

A few tribes moved west without any trouble, but others did not want to leave their homes. By 1835, President Andrew Jackson sent federal troops to drive the Native Americans west. In a forced march that became known as the "Trail of Tears," the Cherokee were forced from their homes by the U.S. government. During the fall and winter of 1838 and 1839, some 4,000 Cherokee died while marching. Other nations also were forced to move out of their territories.

The Battle of the Little Bighorn was one of the last battles against federal troops in the West. In that battle, combined forces of Native Americans defeated Lieutenant Colonel George Custer and his troops.

Preserving the Heritage

Yet despite the brutal journey, broken treaties, and battles, Native American nations today have kept their heritage, and many continue to practice their traditions. In 2014, President Barack Obama visited North Dakota and the **reservation** of the Standing Rock Sioux Tribal Nation, committing the government to more policies to aid in education and other issues.

THE DISAPPEARANCE OF THE BISON

As the **frontier** was settled, the impact of the white settlers hunting the bison, or the American buffalo, affected the Plains Native Americans. Plains Native Americans had hunted the herds for centuries, and were dependent on them for food and clothing materials. At one time, about 60 million bison roamed the country. The herds were close to extinction by 1890. At one point, there may have been only 25 bison remaining in the wild.

In the early 1900s, the American Bison Society was formed to protect and reintroduce the bison. There are about 500,000 bison today, many living on ranches and raised like livestock. There are about 20,000 bison living as herds in the wild.

Native American nations today have kept their heritage and history alive.

Plains Native Americans hunted bison herds for centuries.

Settled Land

The completion of the **transcontinental** railroad brought about big changes in the West. The last spike, a golden one, was driven in Promontory, Utah, in May of 1869, connecting the Union Pacific tracks to the Central Pacific tracks.

American and Chinese railroad employees worked together as they blasted the way for rail tracks through the mountains.

The trips that the pioneers took in covered wagons could now be covered in about six days instead of six months or more. Heavy goods and food could be shipped west easily by train. The railroad had ushered in more immigrants to build it as well, including Chinese workers.

By 1890, the U.S. government in its census, or population count, declared the frontier was settled. The census showed the population as 62,948,000.

Driving the last spike of the transcontinental railroad was celebrated all over the country.

Old West Lives!

This was also when popular culture began to romanticize the "Old West," which means to make it glamorous for people who had never experienced it.

Spreading this view were wild west shows, more than 150 of them traveled across the country. The most famous was Buffalo Bill's Wild West show, led by William F. Cody. The showman traveled around America and Europe, presenting a picture of the Old West from the white settlers' viewpoints.

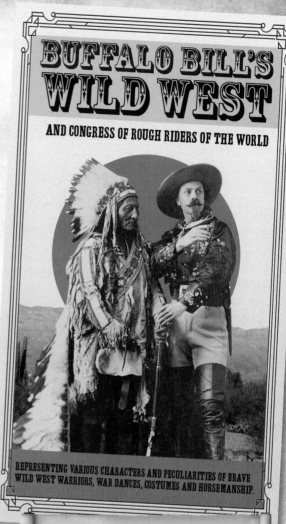

Many posters advertised Buffalo Bill's Wild West show in America and Europe.

MEET BUFFALO BILL

William F. Cody, known as Buffalo Bill by all, made news headlines around the world.

Although there was no social media like today, this frontiersman-hunter-turned-showman got as much publicity as Hollywood stars do now. A guide and scout during the days of westward expansion, he turned his real western experiences into a show. His "Buffalo Bill's Wild West show" re-enacted a vision of the West, including battles between cowboys and Native American nations.

Before he started his show, he worked for the U.S. Army, primarily as a scout. Cody got his nickname after the American Civil War when he had a contract to supply Kansas Pacific Railroad workers with buffalo meat. It is believed that Cody killed 4,282 American bison in eighteen months to supply the meat. He also was a businessman and a developer, founding the town in Wyoming that bears his name, Cody.

Although he was at times criticized for an unfair picture of Native Americans, his contributions made an impact and shaped the identity of the West.

Glossary

claim In pioneer times, this mainly referred to homesteading and owning land. In gold rush terms, a gold prospector could stake a claim, which showed the prospector had a right to work a site.

frontier The edge of land or region that has been settled and inhabited. In United States history, it usually refers to the western United States on the edge of unexplored wilderness by settlers.

homesteading Building a home, or homestead, on unfarmed land that was offered in the 1862 Homestead Act.

ordinance A law or rule set by a governmental body or authority.

pioneers People who were first. In America's westward expansion, the pioneers were the first to explore and settle the frontier.

prairie In the United States, land that is mainly without trees, but covered with grasses.

reservation Land that the United States federal government reserved, or set aside, for Native American nations, after the tribes were removed from their former homelands.

settlement A group of homes and buildings that make up a community in a new region that was not settled earlier.

territory The area of land and water in a particular region.

transcontinental From coast to coast, across the continent of North America.

treaty A pact or agreement between peoples or nations.

westward expansion Moving westward to settle land all the way to the Pacific Ocean, expanding the boundaries of the United States.

For More Information

Further Reading

Domnauer, Teresa. *Westward Expansion*. Scholastic, 2010.

Fieldman, Mel. *The California Gold Rush*. Children's Press, 2010.

Huey Lois. *American Archaeology Uncovers the Westward Movement*. Marshall Cavendish, 2010.

Websites

Due to the changing nature of Internet links, PowerKids Press has developed an online list of websites related to the subject of this book. This site is updated regularly. Please use this link to access the list: **www.powerkidslinks.com/ahac/west**

Index

A

Alabama 7
Alamo 13
American Revolution 4,
    7
Appalachian Mountains
    4, 6

B

Battle of the Little
    Bighorn 26
bison 23, 27, 29
Bonaparte, Napoleon 10
Boone, Daniel 6, 7
Buffalo Bill 29

C

California 5, 13, 18,
    20
Cherokee 26
Clark, William 11, 14
Cumberland Gap 6

F

Florida 4, 5, 7

G

Gold Rush 18
Great Britain 4, 5

H

Homestead Act 22

J

Jefferson, President
    Thomas 10, 11

K

King Louis XIV 10

L

Lewis, Meriwether
    11, 14
Louisiana 5, 10

M

Marshall, James W. 18
Mexico 5, 12, 13
Mississippi 4, 7, 11, 26
Mississippi River 4,
    11, 26
Missouri 14

N

Native American(s) 4,
    5, 7, 11, 15, 23,
    24, 26, 27, 29
New Orleans 10

O

Oregon Trail 14, 15

P

pioneers 6, 15, 19,
    28
Proclamation of 1763
    4, 6

R

Revolutionary War 4,
    7
Rocky Mountains 14

S

Sacagawea 11
Santa Anna, Antonio
    López de 12, 13
settlers 5, 7, 12, 23, 24

T

Texas 4, 5, 12, 13
transcontinental
    railroad 28
Treaty of Paris 7

U

Utah 13, 28